I0148717

Abel Heywood & Son, John F. Mathews

Old south-east Lancashire.

Abel Heywood & Son, John F. Mathews

Old south-east Lancashire.

ISBN/EAN: 9783743328211

Manufactured in Europe, USA, Canada, Australia, Japa

Cover: Foto ©ninafisch / pixelio.de

Manufactured and distributed by brebook publishing software
(www.brebook.com)

Abel Heywood & Son, John F. Mathews

Old south-east Lancashire.

VOL. I.   JANUARY, 1880.   No. 1.

OLD

9-4036

SOUTH-EAST

ROCHDALE.
BURY.
BOLTON

LANCASHIRE

OLDHAM.

ASHTON &
STALYBRIDGE

SALFORD   MANCHESTER

CONCILIO ET LABORE   INTEGRITY & INDUSTRY

A NEW

𝔄𝔯𝔠𝔥𝔞𝔬𝔩𝔬𝔤𝔦𝔠𝔞𝔩, 𝔥𝔦𝔰𝔱𝔬𝔯𝔦𝔠𝔞𝔩, 𝔞𝔫𝔡 𝔊𝔢𝔫𝔢𝔞𝔩𝔬𝔤𝔦𝔠𝔞𝔩 𝔐𝔬𝔫𝔱𝔥𝔩𝔶 𝔐𝔞𝔤𝔞𝔷𝔦𝔫𝔢,

*ESTABLISHED JANUARY, 1880, AS A LOCAL REPRESENTATIVE MEDIUM
FOR ALL WHO, CONJOINTLY WITH ITS PROMOTER AND EDITOR, ARE
INTERESTED IN THE ADVANCEMENT OF LOCAL RESEARCH AND INQUIRY,
OR ARE DESIROUS OF ILLUSTRATING AND DESCRIBING, IN ITS PAGES,
THE RESULTS OF THEIR OWN INDIVIDUAL LABOURS.*

LABORE OMNIA VINCIT   ABSQUE LAB~E MIHI   FRED. ?IGND.

LONDON AND MANCHESTER: ABEL HEYWOOD & SON.
MANCHESTER: JOHN HEYWOOD.   CHESTER: MINSHULL & HUGHES.
WARRINGTON: PEARSE.   BOLTON: WINTERBURN.
AND ALL BOOKSELLERS THROUGHOUT LANCASHIRE AND CHESHIRE.

CONTENTS OF No. 1.

JANUARY, 1880.

OUR TITLE:
WHAT'S IN A NAME?

IN Lancashire, a person is often reluctantly obliged to acknowledge an *alias* when his patronym, for some cogent reason, or probably for some very flimsy or unassignable reason, is denied him by his re-baptisers. In some such manner our county politicians re-christened the Hundred of Salford, and although in legal circles the quondam title is still maintained, the territory is now generally identified under its Parliamentary *alias* of "South-East Lancashire," which *alias*, with an antiquarian prefix, we have adopted as the title of our new magazine. We confess that we should, if questioned, experience some difficulty in assigning a reason for making a selection, which may seem prejudicial to the dignity of the ancient hundred and its time-honoured name. We might, of course, urge that the Census Commissioners, for example, for their purposes ignore the hundreds as territorial distinctions, but we decline to endorse their policy. We might be expected to advance the plea that under a modern title we shall be privileged to treat "Salford Hundret" as a kind of fossil, but we have no desire to dispose of it in that fashion. On the contrary, we seek to honour the ancient territory topographically and archæologically, and shall not, by any means, treat its ancient title as an obsolete term, or the territory as an effete geographical expression. We have much to say of and concerning Salford Hundred, as it was, and not as it is—its Parishes, its Townships, and its byegone worthies. If we do so with an honest purpose, and succeed in securing the friendly counsel and co-operation of fellow labourers, we presume our readers will not quarrel with us upon a point of baptism, seeing that it is our prerogative to christen our hobby according to our own fancy. After all, what's in a name? Our new magazine, by any other name, would fulfil its archæological, historical, and genealogical mission equally well.

"Enquire, I pray thee, of the former age, and prepare thyself to the search of their fathers."—*Job* viii. 8.

COMPLETE LIST*

OF

MEMBERS OF PARLIAMENT FOR LANCASHIRE AND THE SEVERAL BOROUGHS WITHIN THE COUNTY, FROM THE YEAR 1295 TO THE PRESENT TIME.

COMPILED BY J. F. MATTHEWS.

EXISTING Records show that during the half century which preceded the general comprehension of the regeneratory element representatives from all the Cities and Boroughs in England—on the occasion of the meeting of the "First House of Commons," Writs had been occasionally issued requiring the Sheriffs to send representatives from all or some Counties and Boroughs to certain Parliaments, or to Parliaments summoned for certain specified purposes. In the year 1213 (15th King John) Writs were addressed to all the Sheriffs, requiring them to send all the Knights of their Bailiwicks in arms, and also four Knights from their Counties, "ad loquendum nobiscum de negotiis regni nostri," but as no Returns or names can be found relating to the Parliament thus summoned to meet at Oxford on the 15th of November of that year, it cannot now be ascertained whether Lancashire was then represented. It appears that no Writ was issued to the Sheriff of Lancashire in the year 1226 (10th Henry II.), when the mission of the Knights who assembled in the Parliament summoned to meet at Lincoln on the 22nd September in that year, as the elect of the "Milites et probi homines" of Gloucester, Dorset and Somerset,† Bedford and Bucks†, Westmoreland, Northampton, and Lincoln—four from each County—was to set forth their disputes with the Sheriffs as to certain articles of their Charter of Liberty. Writs were issued in the year 1254 (38th Henry III.), requiring every Sheriff to send two Knights, to be elected by each County, "vice omnium et singulorum eorundem ad providendum quale Auxilium‡ nobis in tanta necessitate impendere voluerint," to the Parliament summoned to meet at Westminster on 26th April of the same year, but there is no existing record to show that Lancashire was then represented. With respect to the Parliament summoned to meet at Windsor on the 21st September, 1261 § (45th Henry III.), it may be mentioned that the Bishop of Worcester, the Earl of Leicester, and other magnates, having ordered three Knights from each County to attend an Assembly at St. Albans on 21st September of that year, "secum tractaturi super communibus negotiis regni," and the same day having been appointed by the King for a meeting between himself and those same magnates at Windsor, "ad tractandum de pace inter nos et ipsos," the

---

* Complete so far as the Writs and Returns preserved in the Public Record Office and Crown Office, and all other discovered public and private records, afford reliable data.

† One writ seems to have then sufficed for Dorset and Somerset, and one for Bedford and Bucks.

‡ Aid required towards carrying on the war in Gascony against the King of Castile.

§ The "Mad Parliament" met at Oxford, in 1258.

King enjoined the Sheriffs to send the same Knights also to him at Windsor, "supra præmissis colloquium habituri," but as the Returns and names for that Parliament are missing it cannot be stated, otherwise than doubtfully, whether Lancashire was represented on the occasion. The Writs for the Parliament summoned to meet at London, on the 20th January, 1264-5 (49th Henry III.), required the Sheriffs of Counties and the Cities of York and Lincoln, and the other Boroughs of England, to send two Knights, Citizens, or Burgesses respectively, and the Barons, &c., of each of the Cinque Ports were required to send four men. Notwithstanding the previous issue of casual Writs, and the practical character of the Returns made thereto, the Parliamentary Assembly of the year 1264-5 is historically reckoned as the "First House of Commons," or first Parliament, in which elected Knights, Citizens, and Burgesses sat as the "Third Estate of the Realm." Unfortunately, no official Returns to the Writs of that period remain to show the names of those members who represented Lancashire and its Boroughs in that august body. That Lancashire was represented thereat need scarcely be doubted, as it is on record that a Writ was issued to the Sheriff of this County. For the Parliament summoned to meet at Westminster on the 13th October, 1275 (3rd Edward I.), a solitary Return (without date) for the County of Kent is alone forthcoming. No Return whatever, or names, can be found of the members who constituted the Parliament summoned to meet on the 20th January, 1282-3 (11th Edward I.), at Northampton for the Counties "South of Trent," and at York for those "North of Trent." Four Knights were required to be sent to that Parliament from each County, and two men from each City, Borough, and Market Town, but the Returns are all missing. The Writs for the Parliament summoned to meet at Shrewsbury on 30th September, 1283 (11th Edward I.), required that two Knights be sent from each County, and two Citizens or Burgesses from London and twenty other Cities and Boroughs, but all the Returns are missing, except one for the County of Gloucester, which appears to relate to that Parliament. The Writs issued for the Parliament summoned to meet at Westminster, on 15th July, 1290 (18th Edward I.), required that "two or three" Knights be sent from each County. The Return (which is without date) is the first existing record of its kind which supplies details. It gives the names of members returned for 28 Counties of England, but no Returns can be found to the Writs issued to the Sheriffs of the other Counties, including Lancashire. Two sets of Writs seem to have been issued in 1294, the first set requiring that two Knights be sent from each County, and the second set that "two more" be sent from each County, to the Parliament summoned to meet at Westminster on the 12th November of that year, but the Returns are not forthcoming, and names are wanting.

The first mention of names of elected members returned as representatives of the County of Lancaster and the Boroughs of Lancaster, Liverpool, Preston, and Wigan, is made with respect to the Parliament of the year 1295 (23rd Edw. I.). Two Knights were returned from this County, and two from each of those Boroughs, to serve in the Parliament summoned to meet at Westminster on the 13th, and (by prorogation) on the 27th November, 1295.

Although the official Returns are missing, we are enabled, from a reliable source, to supply the names of the members who sat in that Parliament for Lancashire, and for Lancaster, Liverpool, Preston, and Wigan. They are taken from Transcripts * of Returns from Originals formerly in the Old Office of the King's Remembrancer, but the date of the Returns cannot be ascertained. It is, therefore, all but manifest that during the period of about three-quarters of a century which preceded the year 1295 Writs were issued, and Returns made, for this County, if not for the four ancient Borough constituencies named, but in consequence of the absence of the official data, and the fruitless results of the search for other reliable authorities, we are obliged to commence the following list of names from the year 1295. †   From the latter year until the Parliament of 1477-8 the names of County members have been obtained with tolerable satisfaction, but between the last-named Parliament and that of 1529, or a period of about 52 years, *all* Returns (Lancashire and its Boroughs inclusive) are missing. From 1529 up to the Long Parliament the intervals between elections widened. During the Interregnum an assembly nominated by Oliver Cromwell and a Council of Officers, and summoned by Letters under the hand of Lord General Cromwell, met at Westminster 4th July, 1653, and declared itself a Parliament on the 6th of the same month, but on the 12th of December of the same year it resigned its powers to their originator. For 1654 the Returns for Lancashire are missing. In 1656 four County members were returned. For the Parliaments of 1658-9 and 1660 no Returns can be found for the County or any of its Boroughs, except three relating to Liverpool, Preston, and Wigan for the Parliament of 1660. From the Restoration the representation of the County has been regularly maintained, and members' names preserved uninterruptedly until the present time. Previous to the passing of the Reform Act of 1832 the total number of members returned from Lancashire was fourteen, namely, two for the County, two for each of the ancient Boroughs of Lancaster, Liverpool, Preston, and Wigan, and two for each of the less ancient Boroughs of Clitheroe and Newton. Under the powers of that Act, and for parliamentary election purposes, the County was territorially sectioned into "North Lancashire" and "South Lancashire," and the right of returning one member granted to each Division, making a total of four County

---

* See Palgrave's Calendar of Parliamentary Writs, Vol. I., p. i., &c.

† The question of early representation involves another, equally, if not supremely important, namely, the precise period when Saxon "Loncaster-scyre," which after the Conquest was by Doomsday Book territorially treated as a kind of "no man's land," partly in "Cestre-scire" [Cheshire] and partly in "Euric-scire" [Yorkshire] was re-constituted a distinct County. In solving the latter question—to which, it is to be hoped, attention will be directed by some writer in a separate article in a future number of this Magazine—the fact that on several occasions previous to the year 1295 two or three and sometimes four Knights were required to be sent to the English Parliament from certain specified Counties, and at other times from each County, should be kept steadily in view. In 1363 Lancashire was permanently raised anew to the dignity of a County Palatine, a previous temporary elevation to that honour having lapsed.

members. Pursuant to the provisions of the "Representation of the People Act, 1867," the County was re-sectioned into four Divisions, which were named "North Lancashire" (embracing the Hundreds of Lonsdale, Amounderness, and Leyland); "North East Lancashire" (embracing the Hundred of Blackburn); "South East Lancashire" (co-extensive with the Hundred of Salford); and "South West Lancashire" (comprising the Hundred of West Derby), and the right of returning two members conceded to each Division, in the same manner as to, Counties.

LANCASTER BOROUGH. [First chartered by King John.] As will be seen on reference to subsequent monthly sections of this list, the privilege of returning two members exercised by Lancaster in and probably previous to the year 1295 (23rd Edward I.), was suspended after the Parliament of the year 1331 (5th Edward III.), and from that time Lancaster remained unrepresented up to the year 1529 (21st Henry VIII.), when the elective right was renewed. Thereafter, with the exception of some interruptions, and temporary suspensions which occurred between the years 1603-4 and 1661, and which will be found detailed in their order of date in the list, the renewed right of representation was continuously enjoyed until the passing of the Second Reform Act of 1867, when the Borough was disfranchised for bribery.

LIVERPOOL BOROUGH. [First chartered by King John.] The right of representation in Parliament by two members dates from the year 1295, probably earlier. After the Parliament of 1306-7 the right was wholly suspended at Liverpool—then a mere fishing station—until the Parliament summoned to meet at Westminster on the 4th November, 1547. With the exception of a few temporary suspensions (hereafter noticed) Liverpool continued to be represented by two members until the passing of "The Representation of the People Act, 1867," when the vastly-increased constituency was empowered to return three members, and that number is presently returnable.

PRESTON BOROUGH. [First chartered by Henry II., and the recipient of 13 subsequent Royal charters.] From the year 1295, if not from an earlier date, until the year 1331 Preston returned two members, but for the space of nearly 200 years—from the latter year until the Parliament of 1529—this right was wholly suspended. In 1529 the constituency is described in the Records as "Preston-in-Alderness Borough," but five years later it is referred to as "Preston-in-Amounderness Borough." With the exception of some temporary suspensions between the beginning of the 17th century and the time of the Restoration, Preston continuously exercised the right of returning two members to Parliament from the year 1529 to the present time. At Preston, from time immemorial, the right of voting on the occasions of parliamentary elections was, previous to the Act of 1832, vested in all male inhabitants of the age of twenty-one years and upwards who had resided six months within the Borough, and had not for twelve months immediately preceding an election been chargeable to any parish as paupers. The right was left undisturbed by the Reform Acts of 1832 and 1867 so far as pre-existent voters were concerned, and it is still exercisable by the few survivors who remain.

WIGAN BOROUGH. [First chartered by Henry III.] Writs were issued to and Returns made from Wigan in 1295, and probably before that date, but previous Returns and names are missing. After the Parliament of 1306-7 the exercise of the right of representation ceased for 240 years. In 1547 the elective right was renewed, and, with the exception of temporary suspensions and interruptions similar to those which affected the other ancient Boroughs of the County, Wigan continued to return two members to Parliament from that year until the present time.

CLITHEROE. [A Borough by prescription.] The Return to the first Writ for this Borough is dated 13th January, 1558-9 (1st Elizabeth). Under the authority of the mandate the Burgesses returned two members from Clitheroe to serve in the Parliament summoned to meet at Westminster on the 23rd of that month, and from that time the elective right continued to be exercised — but not uninterruptedly—until the passing of the first Reform Act of 1832, when the Borough was deprived of one member. In the earlier records Clitheroe took precedence of the other Lancashire Boroughs from the date of its enfranchisement until the passing of that Act. It still returns one member.

NEWTON-LE-WILLOWS or Newton-in-Makerfield. [A Borough by prescription.] This constituency—never large—was anciently the head of a Barony. It received its elective franchise in the year 1558. The Return to the first Writ is dated 7th January, 1558-9 (1st Elizabeth), and according to it two members were returned to the Parliament summoned to meet at Westminster on the 23rd of the same month. Newton was at that time described as " The Borough of Sir Thomas Langton, Knt., Baron of Newton within his Fee of Markerfylde." Forty-five years later it was referred to as "Newton-in-Makerfield Borough." The representatives who sat in the Parliament summoned to meet in 1620-1 are described as having been " elected with the consent of Sir Richard Fleetwood, Lord of the Borough." Its elective franchise was occasionally disturbed or temporarily suspended after the Long Parliament, but immediately after the Restoration the Borough resumed the exercise of its former right, and from that period it continued to return two members to each Parliament until the passing of the Reform Act of 1832, when it was disfranchised.

MANCHESTER. [Constituted a free Borough by charter, granted by Thomas Gresley, 14th May, 1301. Elevated to the dignity of a City in 1847.] The return to the (first) Writ for " Manchester Borough," issued in 1654 by the Lord Protector of the Commonwealth, Oliver Cromwell, to the High Sheriff, cannot be found, but it is on record that in obedience to the mandate the Burgesses of Manchester returned Charles Worsley to serve in the Parliament which met at Westminster on the 3rd September, 1654. " The House," proving refractory, was dismissed by Cromwell on the 22nd January, 1654-5.* In the year 1656 a fresh Cromwellian Writ was issued, requiring the Sheriff to return one representative for Manchester. The Return, which is dated 12th August, 1656, was torn when found, but enough remained to show that

---

* Until 1752 the English year was reckoned to end on the 24th of March.

" —— ' Radcliffe, Esq., of Manchester," was the elect sent to the Parliament which met at Westminster on the 17th of September, 1656. This Parliament having, amongst other things, proposed some changes in the Government, was itself dissolved 4th February, 1657-8. No Returns can be found for the Parliament of 1658-9. On the decline of the "Roundhead" power, the temporary right of representation thrust upon Manchester ceased, and was not renewed until sanctioned by the Reform Act of 1832, when the Borough was again enfranchised and privileged to return two members. Under the powers of the "Representation of the People Act, 1867," Manchester was invested with the right of returning three members to the Imperial Parliament, a privilege still exercised.

SALFORD. Enfranchised by the first Reform Act of 1832, and privileged to return one member. The Act of 1867 gave the Borough an additional member. Two are now returned.

BOLTON, BLACKBURN, and OLDHAM were enfranchised by the Act of 1832, and privileged to return two members each.

ASHTON-UNDER-LYNE, BURY, ROCHDALE, and WARRINGTON were enfranchised by the same Act, which granted to each Borough the right of representation by one member.

STALYBRIDGE (partly in Cheshire) and BURNLEY were enfranchised by "The Representation of the People Act, 1867," and received the privilege of returning one member each.

By these changes the representative strength of the County and its Boroughs was increased to 33 members, the number presently returnable.

In the first column of the following list the name of the sovereign and year of reign are given; in the second and third columns the place at which and the date upon which each Parliament was summoned to meet; in the fourth the date of the Return ;† and in the last column will be found the names of the members returned to serve in Parliament for Lancashire and the several Boroughs within the County. The ambiguity which characterises names given in ancient records and documents is nowhere more provokingly illustrated than in some of the originals from which the following information was gleaned. Many of the names appear to have been Gallicized or Latinized alternately, just as the scribe's fancy prompted or his pedantry urged. It will also be observed from the list that frequently the spelling "waxes wanton," and betimes, regardless of orthographic bounds, romps about as unrestrainedly as in the "good old times" of Chaucer. No attempt has been made to spoil the antiqueness of the names, or their spelling, by modernizing them.

The preparation of the subjoined list was commenced several years ago, and the work of collection of the materials has been assiduously prosecuted since, as opportunity offered, often under many disadvantages, at considerable outlay for searches and information, and all the while in ignorance of the sparsely-known

---

* Richard Radcliffe was the member elected.

† This column will be introduced at a later stage of the list, such dates not being given in earlier years.

B

fact that the House of Commons had, on 4th May, 1876, ordered the preparation of an elaborate Return, so far as it could be obtained, from the year 1696 to the present time, and by a further Order dated 9th March, 1877, directed that the Return should be extended back " from as remote a period as it can be obtained up to the year 1696." Recently, since the issue of the voluminous Blue Book to the " House," an early copy came to the hands of the writer of these prefatory remarks. In it he found some materials which he had been long in search of, and which enabled him to complete his labours satisfactorily and to present them in the following form to the reader.

NOTE.—Where the Original Returns are missing, the names given have been supplied from an independent authority. To names thus obtained an asterisk is attached throughout the list.

Sovereign and year of reign.	Place at which, and date upon which each Parliament was summoned to meet.		Members returned.
23 Edwd. I.	Westminster	13th & 27th Nov., 1295.	COUNTY:— Mattheus de Redman. Johannes de Ewyas. LANCASTER BOROUGH:— Lambertus le Despenser. Willielmus le Chaunter. LIVERPOOL BOROUGH:— Adam fil' Richardi. Robertus Pynklowe. PRESTON BOROUGH:— Willielmus fil' Pauli. Adam Russel. WIGAN BOROUGH: Willielmus le Teinterer. Henricus le Bocher.
24 „	Bury St. Edmunds	3rd Nov., 1296.	(No returns found).
25 „	(a) London	6th Oct., 1297.	COUNTY:— Henricus de Kigheleye. Henricus de Botiler.
26 „	York	25th May, 1298.	COUNTY:— Henricus de Kigheley'. Johannes Denyas. LANCASTER BOROUGH:— Rudulphus fil' Thome. Willielmus de Chauntour. PRESTON BOROUGH:— Adam fil' Radulfi. Adame de Biri.
28 „	†London or Westminster	6th March, 1299-1300.	COUNTY:— *Gilbertus de Sengleton'. *Robertus de Haydok'.
„ „	(b) York	20th May, 1300	(No return for Lancashire or any of its boroughs found.)

(a) Two Knights to be sent from each County.
† No original writs for this Parliament except Yorkshire.
(b) Summoned concerning the observation of " Magna Carta et Carta de Foresta." Three Knights or others to be sent from each county.

(To be continued.)

1816.

(Copied by Mr. Wm. Moss from a sketch of the period by Mr. James Bury, of Bolton.)

1879.

(From a Sketch by Mr. William Moss, of Bolton.)

A RELIC OF OLD BOLTON.

[SEE ILLUSTRATIONS.]

CONCERNING the old relic, the subject of the pair of engravings on the preceding page, it was said recently by a local architectural utilitarian—one who admitted, however, that he derives much pleasure while delineating many choice features in the antiquities of Bolton—that with the closest scrutiny, he could not find any feature of interest in it; that there was not even a moulding, or bit of detail worth remembering; that simply nothing existed but its picturesque grouping of gables, and that these and the "queer old ruin, he, for one, should not miss." While admiring his candour, and admitting that a portion of his allegation was strictly true, we should, perhaps, be considered false to our mission did we not seek to discover better evidence, and with it the remainder of the truth. Allegorically we put "Antiquarian" in the witness box, and a further instalment of the truth was elicited in favour of Madame Wood and Plaster. This witness who was indignant at the previous witness's lack of antiquarian enthusiasm, after rating him soundly for his sins of omission and commission, and quoting the sentiments of Livy and Macaulay with respect to the study of antiquity, warmly expressed his own opinion that many vivid associations surrounded the old fabric. A third witness expressed a belief that from an architectural point of view, this bit of old Bolton was worthless; and after assigning really cogent reasons against the groundless assumptions of others that it was once Bradshaw Hall, or that its erection dated from the year 1517, declared that it would, he thought, be a bit nearer the mark if we said the middle of the sixteenth century, and ended by pleading that necessity demanded its demolition. The evidence of a fourth witness went to prove the antiquarian value of this Bradshaw-gate relic, and the advisability of saving it as the focus of many associations connected with the history of Bolton. One sterling quality, in two separate aspects, he demonstrated, namely, the simplicity of the edifice on one hand, and on the other, the true nobility who, in turn, figured as its primitive owners, occupiers, or guests. The last witness alone approached the subject of associations earnestly, but he fell short in his praiseworthy research, and therefore failed to disclose a tithe of the underlying facts. Who among these allegoried witnesses (correspondents through the local press), or who among their readers dreamt that intimately connected with the old building were many who figure prominently in local history? Closely connected with it are the names of Thomas Lever, Esq., of Chamber Hall, governor-elect for Bolton in 1672, of Chetham Hospital, Manchester, and benefactor to the poor and school of Bolton; Mrs. Blackburne, of Orford, his daughter, a benefactress to the church and poor of Bolton; John Blackburne, of Orford, her son, and inheritor of the estates of his grandfather (the same Thomas Lever), afterwards lord of the manor of Warrington by purchase, and eminently known as the Evelyn of his day; Oliver Heywood, the divine; Rev. John Lever, the ejected curate of Cockey Chapel; his three daughters, Misses Lydia, Martha, and Elizabeth Lever, who, in their day, were "alike eminent for a grave and modest deportment, for personal charms and intellectual endowments, called by the swains of that age, the "flowers of Bolton,"* and by their poorer neighbours, "the fine ladies of Bradshaw-gate," or "the white-aproned ladies :"† Peter Dorning, "a man of respectable connections and character," who within those old walls wooed and won Miss Lydia Lever ; Rev. Joseph Heywood‡ (son of Oliver), who in like manner won her sister, Miss Martha ; Robert Dunn, whose prize was their sister, Miss Elizabeth ; Rev. John Lever, Vicar of Bolton, who lived on terms of amity with his namesake, their father, and "used to walk up and down the town with him arm in arm :¶ John Dorning of Farnworth, chapman, son of Peter and Lydia, who in 1743 bought the old homestead from John Blackburne for £87 ; Sarah Dorning, his sister ; Dorning Rasbotham, cousin of John and Sarah Dorning, a resident magistrate, who, amongst other MSS., preserved a list of the prices of provisions in Bolton in the year 1745, and for forty-two years afterwards, and who probably wrote much of his manuscript within those old walls where he was always welcome, and of which he in his turn became the inheritor : and last, though not least, "our mutual friend" Parson Folds, after whom the tributary street which bounded the old residence on the north side (formerly called Lever-street), was named Fo ds-street.†† These are facts which utilitarians cannot dispose of with a fillip, nor evade when thrust home with a kindly wish. At the risk of crushing out other important matter we proceed to submit our unavoidably lengthy, but we trust interesting, munimentary evidence as to former proprietorship of the venerable old premises.

Title deeds now in the hands of Thomas Walmsley, Esq., J.P., Bolton, and Brooklyn, Great Lever, have enabled us to trace back the ownership of this venerable old wood and plaster "messuage, burgage, or dwelling-house" to the year 1680, or two hundred years ago. Mr. Walmsley having kindly granted our written request for permission to inspect the documents, we promptly availed ourselves of the offer, and on the 29th of November last journeyed to

---

* Relation of conversations with Mrs. Betty Chapman, of Little Bolton, then aged 79, great great granddaughter of Oliver Heywood, and great granddaughter to Rev. John Lever. *Brown's History of Great and Little Bolton,* an extremely rare work.

† Appellatives denoting that in the reign of William III., or Queen Anne, a white linen apron was considered as a mark of dignity.

‡ After his ordination he came on a visit to the house of some friend in Bolton, and being a handsome young man, his friend said to him, "Do you want a good wife? If you do, I can introduce you where you may find one." His friend being a grave kind of person, Parson Heywood took him at his word, and he introduced him to the daughters of the Rev. John Lever, who resided with an old housekeeper of their deceased father, "in a house in Bradshaw-gate, near where the public-house, the sign of the 'Fleece,' then stood." The father died in 1692, and according to our venerable informant, in very good circumstances, leaving each of his three daughters a good portion. Vide Brown's relation of Mrs. Chapman's statements.

¶ Mrs. Chapman's relation to Brown the historian.

†† Diary of the father of Thomas Holden, Esq., Registrar of the Bolton County Court·

his residence, where, besides finding the deeds and their owner " at home," we found ourselves honoured as the welcome recipients of his genial hospitality. Having, on turning over the deeds, ascertained that a lease and a release, dated 1st and 2nd June, 1743, were the earliest among them, we turned the release open, in expectation of finding recitals of older deeds, but we were disappointed. Near the end of the deed, however, embodied in a heterogeneous covenant against incumbrances, we alighted upon an out-of-the-way reference to a pre-existent lease, which to some extent compensated us for the disappointment experienced on opening the deed. From that covenant we learned that in 1680 the premises—of which the old relic now forms a part—were owned by one " Thomas Lever," but the clause in which the name occurs afforded no description whatever of the individual so called, by which his identification could be established. Our reflections at the moment were directed to the only propertied person of that name, connected with Bolton and that period, whose locale and position warranted the assumption that he was owner in 1680 of the premises in question. We refer to Thomas Lever, Esq., who was elected, in 1672, governor for Bolton of Chetham Hospital, Manchester. His name appeared as such in an old memorial list painted upon a board or tablet formerly within Bolton Old Church, headed " To the Memory of Humfrey Chetham, Esqr., Founder of the Hospital and Library in Manchester, A.D. 1651," &c., and purporting to be a complete list of the governors for Bolton and Turton of that institution, up to and inclusive of the year 1737. We were also aware that upon another old board or painted tablet, also formerly within the same old church, headed " The names of the Benefactors to the Church, Poor, and School of Bolton," the name and address, " Thomas Lever, Esq., of Bolton,' appeared, opposite the date " 1704," in connection with two benefactions by him—£30 to the poor, and £30 to the schools. Subsequent research confirmed our conjecture that lessor, governor, and benefactor were one and the same individual. Thomas Lever, Esq., then of Chamber Hall, was the Bolton worthy whose name figures in the covenant mentioned. He died in the 80th year of his age, and was interred † within the Old Church on the 21st of August, 1704—a date which, it will be observed, corresponds with that of the above-mentioned benefactions. His son and namesake, also described as of Chamber Hall, who died in 1679, aged 25, could not, of course, have been the lessor named in a deed dated in 1680. The covenant referred to alludes briefly to a lease dated 11th February, 1680, " granted by Thomas Lever " to " John Lever, clerk," of the " messuage, burgage, or dwelling-house," &c., in Bradshawgate

---

† His tombstone was one of those laid bare in 1866, upon the floor of the south aisle of Bolton Old Church, after removal of the high-backed pews which stood nearest to and in front of the old south aisle of the chancel or ancient chapel of the Levers, afterwards of the Bridgmans, and lastly of the Bradford family. It was the most southerly tombstone in the row in which it was found, and lay about ten feet from the old south wall. The following is a copy of the whole of the inscription :— " Thomas Leaver, of Chamber Hall, gentleman, aged 25 years, departed this life the 10th and was here interred the 13th Decr., Anno Doma 1679. Thomas Leaver, Esq., was here interred 21st day of August, 1704, being the 80th year of his age."

subsequently granted by the deed which contains such covenant", for the term
of " the naturall and severall life and lives of Lidia, Martha, and Elizabeth
daughters of the said John Lever, and of the survivor of them, under the
yearly rent of four shillings and eight pence," the same rent to grow " due and
payable unto the said John Dorning" [the grantee or purchaser named in the
earliest existing title deed, next described]. " his heirs and assigns, during the
continuance of the said lease" of 1680". Lydia, daughter of the Rev. John
Lever, one of the lives, became the wife of Peter Dorning, and mother of John
Dorning, who became the purchaser of the Bradshawgate property. She died
12th September, 1711.

The Rev. John Lever ("John Lever, clerk"), the lessee of 1680, must not
be confounded with his clerical namesake and contemporary, the Rev. John
Lever, vicar of the parish of Bolton from the year 1673 to the year 1691
Few Boltonians of the present day are aware that the lessee of 1680 was none
other than the Rev. John Lever, the ejected minister of Cockey Moor Chapel
in the adjoining parish of Middleton, who subsequently succeeded the Rev
Richard Goodwin, the ejected vicar of Bolton, as minister of the congregation
which in those days of non-conformity worshipped at " The Meeting House,"
now part of the Old Wool Pack Inn, in Deansgate, Bolton, and who died 4th July,
1692. He was born in Bolton, and it is believed that the event occurred
in the same " messuage, burgage, or dwelling-house " * of which in 1680
he became the lessee—the relic of which we now write. His tombstone,† to
be seen in Bolton parish churchyard, besides covering the remains of two of

---

* " In 1672 he (Rev. John Lever) preached to a good number in his own house."—
Calamy.

† His tombstone may be seen in Bolton parish churchyard, on the south side of
the new church. A few yards from it—in the thirteenth row from the Old Grammar
School wall, ninth stone from the south side of the church—is the tombstone of his
namesake, the Rev. John Lever, vicar of Bolton, who died 14th October, 1691. The
tombstone of the Rev. John Lever (the lessee) may be easily identified. Besides being
fractured across the middle, its right corner at top is missing, and with it are gone the
ending letters of the first three lines of the first record. The following is a verbatim
copy of the inscription, the words or parts of words within brackets being those
which are missing :—

" Here Lyeth the body [of] Iohn Leaver Borne in th[is] Towne a Faithful Minister
of t[he] Gospel who was baptized the 11 day of September 1631 and departed this life
4 day of July 1692

Lidia his Daughter and Wife to Peter Dorning was here interred the 12th day of
September 1711

Also Elizabeth his Daughter and Wife to Robert Dunn who Departed this life the
10th day of February 1760 In the 82 Year of her Age

Here resteth the Body of John Dorning the Son of Peter and Lydia Dorning of
Bolton who Died the 12th of April 1762 In the 63rd Year of his Age

Here Also resteth the Body of Mary Dunn the Daughter of Elizabeth Dunn who
Departed this life Novr. 3d 1778 aged 76 "

The surname spelled " Leaver " in the inscription, is written " Lever " in the earliest
title deed, and in the latter form it appears in the entry of deceased's burial, in Bolton
parish church register.

the three lives named in the lease of 1680, also covers the remains of some of the previous occupiers and subsequent owners of the old property.

The oldest title deed contains a covenant which shows that in and previous to the year 1713, John Blackburne, of Orford, Esq., "grandson of Thomas Lever" (the before-named lessor of 1680), was absolutely seized of this Bradshawgate property, "as a good, perfect, and indefeasible estate of inheritance in fee simple" This information was the highly serviceable clue by which our subsequent searches were initiated and guided. The mother of John Blackburne (the vendor) was Anne,* daughter of Thomas Lever, relict† of C. Lockwood, Esq., of Leeds, and heiress of Chamber Hall, who (as his second wife) married Jonathan Blackburne, Esq. (born 1646), of Orford and Newton, fourth son of Thomas Blackburne (died 1663, aet suae 58), of Newton, and Margaret, daughter of Robert Norris, of Bolton. They had three sons— Thomas the first, who died in India; John, the second (of whom more presently), and Jonathan, the third son, of whom we need not give account. John, the second son, became by marriage the owner of the old premises in Bradshawgate, the subject of this article, and also became lord of the manor of Warrington, by purchase. He married, at Winwick, Catharine, daughter of the Rev. William Ashton, B.D., rector of Prestwich, and died 20th December, 1796,‡ aet 96. He was the same venerable John Blackburne, Esq.,†† whose scientific pursuits, principally in botany and natural history,❡ made him justly famous, and whose daughter, Mary, inheriting her father's tastes, became, celebrated for her devotion to botanical researches, and her stronger attachment to the study of natural history.

---

* Anne, sister and co-heiress with Sir Darcey Lever's wife, and aunt to Sir Ashton Lever, knight. She died in 1740.

† Burke's Landed Gentry, p. 134.

‡ Baines, vol. ii. p. 233-4 ; Gregson, Foster, and others give the date as 1786, aet 93.

†† The family of Blackburne is of ancient lineage. The origin of the surname is traceable to the name of the turgid burn or stream, which gave its name to the town of Blackburn. The Lancashire branch of the family commenced with William Blackburne, the elder brother of, and partner in trade with, Richard. These two brothers came from Yorkshire, and settled as merchants in the Filde, in an extensive Russian trade, and resided at Thistleton. Richard Blackburne (eldest son of William), first of Scorton Hall, near Garstang, afterwards of Thistleton, and lastly of Newton, married Jane, daughter of John Aynesworth, of Newton. Their third son, Thomas Blackburne, of Orford and Newton (baptised 9th June, 1604), was esteemed a learned man in his time. He had seven sons and nine daughters. The fourth son was Jonathan (named in the text), who became heir of his brother Thomas. "Blackburn"- street in Bolton was named after the Blackburne family, not after the town of that name. The corporation of Bolton should correct their error by adding the final "e" to the word. Crook-street, in the same neighbourhood, was named after the Crooks, a related family.

❡ "It is recorded of this amiable man that he was the second gentleman of England who cultivated the pine apple, and he was probably the first to cultivate the cotton plant to any practical purpose, having raised in his garden at Orford a supply of British cotton, from four ounces of which was made a muslin dress for his lady, with

C

" By indenture, dated 2nd June, 1743, and made in the
sixteenth year of the reign of our Sovereign Lord GEORGE
the Second, of Great Britain, France, and Ireland, King,
Defender of the Faith, &c.," the same John Blackburne, in
consideration of £87, paid, &c., granted, &c., unto John
Dorning,§ of Farnworth, chapman, the old premises under
the description of "ALL THAT Messuage, Burgage, or
Dwelling-house, Backside and Garden, with their and
every of their appurtenances, situate and being in Bolton-
in-the-Moores, in the said county, in a Place or Street
there called Bradshawgate, heretofore in the holding or
occupation of John Lever, clerk, deceased, and late in the
holding or occupation of Peter Dorning, deceased, late
father of the said John Dorning, and now in the possession
of the said John Dorning, his subtenants or assigns," &c.,
TO HOLD, &c., unto the said John Dorning, his heirs and
assigns, &c., for ever. "To BE holden of the Chief Lord
or Lords of the ffee or ffees of the said Premises (if any
such there be), by the Rents and Services therefore due
and of right accustomed," &c.   The handwriting of the
signature, "John Blackburne," is scholarly, bold, free,
and distinct, the Christian name and surname having a
red wax seal between them, the latter bearing the combined arms of Blackburne and Lever. The following are
fac similes of signature and seal:—

The execution by the grantor is attested by two
witnesses:—

"HUGH ENTWISLE.

HENRY MORETON."

the intention to appear at Court in it on the King's birthday in 1793; but a change
of dress, occasioned by the death of a near relative, prevented it. Miss Anna
Blackburne's house, in the immediate vicinity of Warrington, was a perfect museum,
and had to boast some of the finest transatlantic specimens in this kingdom. She
was a correspondent of Linnæus; and a genus of plants was named after her
(*Blackburniana*) by Reinhold Forster, the celebrated naturalist, who accompanied Capt·
Cook in his second voyage, in testimony of her great acquirements in natural history,
and her kindness to him during his abode in Warrington. On her death her collection
was removed to Hale, where it is still preserved."—*Baines*, Vol. III. p. 677.

§ Son of Peter and Lydia Dorning.

On the back of the deed is the following receipt :—

" RECEIVED the day and year first within mentioned, of and from the within-named John Dorning, the sum of Eighty-seven pounds, of lawful money of Great Britain, in full of the consideration within mentioned. As WITNESS my hand, " JOHN BLACKBURNE.

" Signed in the presence of

" HUGH ENTWISLE.

HENRY MORETON."

Within the large initial letter " ℭ " of the engraved ornamental heading or beginning word, " This Indenture," are the royal arms. Outside of and encircling the royal motto, are a name and address, thus, " Sold by S. Gibbons, stationer, near the Temple Church," which to us served as a hint that in those days deed parchment and deed stamps needed by Bolton lawyers required to be imported from the metropolis. The price of the parchment was indicated in the margin at foot by a crown and " S 12d.," within a half-inch circle—rather a large figure for a skin of a small size, considering the value of twelve pence at that period.

It will be observed that in the description of the premises in the deed of 1743, no mention is made of any street other than Bradshawgate as a boundary. The inference is that the passage or thoroughfare now represented by Folds'-street did not then exist, or was not then named.

By his will, dated 10th April, 1755, John Dorning, the purchaser of 1743, devised " ALL THAT my Messuage and Dwelling House, with the appurtenances, situate, standing, and being in Bolton-in-the-Moors, in the county of Lancaster, now or late in the tenure or occupation of Mr. Timothy Aspinwall, his assigns or undertenants, unto my sister, Sarah Dorning, and her assigns, for and during the term of her natural life, she keeping the same in good repair, and from and after her decease unto my cousin, Dorning Rasbotham, his heirs and assigns, for ever," &c. Of said will testator nominated and appointed his cousin Peter Rasbotham and his sons, Dorning Rasbotham and Nathan Rasbotham, executors. The original will was witnessed by Sarah Kay, John Kay, and Will. Higginson. A codicil annexed, dated 27th March, 1762, which did not affect the disposition made by his will of the Bradshawgate property, is witnessed by one person only—" Richard Mason." A second codicil, not dated, was also added, and signed by the testator, but was not witnessed. Two other sisters of the testator named in his will as legatees, were Hannah Bradshaw and Lydia Hindley. According to the Leaver-Dorning-Dunn tombstone, in Bolton churchyard, John Dorning died in the 63rd year of his age, on the 12th of April, 1762, or in about a fortnight after the date of the first codicil to his will. Upon his death the Bradshawgate premises passed to his sister Sarah (who survived him) for life.

Sarah Dorning died on the   day of   17   , whereupon the premises became legally vested in her (and testator's) cousin, Dorning Rasbotham, " of Birch House, in Farnworth, Esquire."

Dorning Rasbotham,* by his will, dated 19th August, 1791, amongst other things, gave and devised, "ALL my messuages, dwelling-houses, farms, lands, hereditaments, and real estates of inheritance whatsoever, in Farnworth, Great Bolton, and Ashton-in-Mackersfield, with the appurtenances, unto my dearly beloved wife, Sarah Rasbotham, for and during the term of her natural life;" and from and after her decease, he gave and devised the same unto his brother-in-law, James Bayley, of Withington, clerk, Thomas Butterworth Bayley, of Hope, Esq., and James Touchett, of Manchester, merchant, their heirs, executors, administrators, and assigns, for ever UPON TRUST, to sell the same immediately after the decease of his wife, Sarah Rasbotham, and to apply the money arising from such sale in payment of certain bequests directed by his will. The testator died on the 7th November, 1791. His wife, who survived him, and enjoyed the property for over thirteen years, died on the 30th April, 1805. Thomas Butterworth Bayley, one of his trustees, died on the 24th day of June, 1802, at Buxton, in the 58th year of his age.

Upon the death of Mrs. Sarah Rasbotham (testator's widow), Messrs. James Bayley and James Touchett, the surviving trustees, in pursuance of the trusts in them vested under and by the will of Dorning Rasbotham, advertised the deceased's estates for sale, at various dates and at various places, and sold same by auction. Among the properties advertised for sale, and sold on the 29th November, 1805, were the Bradshawgate premises. The advertisement occupied seven-eighths of an entire column of a Manchester newspaper of the period, called *The Manchester Mercury and Harrop's Gene-*

---

* The Rasbothams, who were of Scotch extraction, settled in Lancashire soon after the Battle of Flodden Field. The family name was then spelled Rosbotham. Dorning Rasbotham was born in Manchester in 1730. In 1754 he married Sarah, eldest daughter of James Bayley, Esq., of Withington and Manchester, and granddaughter of Bishop Peploe. Their six children were Anne, who died unmarried; Dorothy, who died in infancy; Peter, who married Dorothy (born 1767), eldest daughter of John Lever, who, in 1778, succeeded to the Alkrington estates of his brother, Sir Ashton Lever; Dorning, who married Sarah, daughter of John Gray, Esq., of Finedon, in Northumberland; and Frances (born 25th August, 1774, died 12th January, 1838), youngest daughter, who became the wife of William Gray (born 15th August, 1774, died 16th September, 1842), Esq., of Wheatfield, in Haulgh, Bolton. Dorning Rasbotham, senior, retired in 1762 from Manchester to Farnworth, and soon after became a presiding Justice of the Peace on the Bolton bench, meanwhile pursuing his literary studies. He died 7th November, 1791, in the 61st year of his age, and was buried in Deane church yard, where also lie the remains of his widow, who survived him nearly 14 years, and died 30th April, 1805, aged 77. A mural tablet in Deane church, erected by their surviving children, bearing a long inscription, perpetuates the memory of "Parents so revered and so dear." On the "Gray" altar monument in Bolton parish church yard there is a touching allusion to the death of Mr. Rasbotham's youngest daughter Frances (Mrs. Gray) in these words:—"Her loss will be sincerely and deeply mourned, not only by her family, but also by her poorest neighbours and a numerous circle of friends and acquaintances, to whom she was endeared by many most amiable qualities and her good life."

ral Advertiser, in which it appeared four successive weeks, namely, on the 5th, 12th, 19th, and 26th November, 1805. Other estates of the deceased, situated elsewhere, were also advertised and sold about the same time. The sale was announced to take place " By order of the trustees under the will of the late Dorning Rasbotham, Esq., at the house of Mrs. Tong, known by the sign of the 'Golden Lion,' at Moses Gate, in Farnworth, in the county of Lancaster, on Friday, the 29th day of November next, at three o'clock in the afternoon, subject to such conditions as will be then and there produced." Nine lots were advertised to be sold on that occasion, comprising eight sets of premises situate in Farnworth (including Birch House, the testator's late residence), and Halshaw Moor, and one set of premises in Bolton. With the latter property alone have we anything to do. Its description was : — " Lot 9. ALL THOSE two several Cottages or Dwelling-Houses, situate in Bradshaw-gate, in Great Bolton, in the said County of Lancaster, together with the vacant land and appurtenances thereto belonging, now in the occupation of James Baron and James Heaton, as tenants thereof respectively from year to year, and containing in the whole by admeasurement (including the site of the buildings), two hundred and eighty-seven superficial square yards of land or thereabouts, be the same more or less." The advertisement ends with :— " Plans of the estates are lodged at the office of Sharpe and Eccles, attornies, in Manchester, where further particulars may be had, and a person is appointed to attend at Birch House to shew the premises. The purchasers of the larger lots (1, 5, and 8) may be accommodated with a part of the purchase money on the security of the premises." It is apparent from the description of the premises as advertised, that some time before the sale the old " messuage, burgage, or dwelling-house," had become converted into " two several cottages or dwelling-houses," but it is evident from the description contained in the deed of 1816 and known facts that an outbuilding in the rere had been converted into a cottage, not that the " messuage " fronting Bradshawgate had been so partitioned and built on. It will be seen from the same deed of 1816 that the carrier's warehouse was erected partly on vacant land and partly upon " the scite of the said two cottages or dwelling-houses." The front " messuage " (afterwards two shops) remained undisturbed by the carrier's modern erection raised westward of it and long ago partly demolished.

Reverting at this stage to the question of the street boundary of the north side of the premises, we think it right to mention that among Mr. Walmsley's documents we observed a carefully preserved plan headed " Premises in Bolton belonging to the late Dorning Rasbotham, Esq., 1805," in which the street now called Folds'-street is distinctly marked " Lever-street "—doubtlessly so called after the Lever family, the original owners. According to that plan the " contents " of Mr. Dorning Rasbotham's Bradshawgate premises were " 287 square yards," bounded on the south by " Premises belonging to Francis Wrigley ; " on the west by other premises of "Francis Wrigley ; " on the east by " Bradshawgate," and on the north by " Lever-street, 8 yards wide." Mr. Walmsley's plan is doubtless a correct copy of that exhibited to intending purchasers and others at the place of sale. The first mention of Folds'-street in the title deeds occurs in the Release of 16th March, 1839, all previous references to street boundary and nomenclature having been made with respect to Bradshawgate only. Our earlier sketch—that of 1816—enables us, with singular perspicuity, to narrow the transitional period when "Lever-street" was changed to "Folds'-street." Throughout the deeds the latter name is spelled variously. If the reader carefully examine the original of the sketch of 1816, exhibited in the Exchange Museum, Town Hall Square, Bolton, he will find that on the Folds'-street gable, on the side next Bradshawgate, the words "Folds'-street" are written in diminutive, but distinct, characters, and that between those two words and the corner, the word "street" appears, but with traces of some erased letters over it, such erasure being, to our mind, an unmistakeable indication of a change of street name. Our engraver, Mr. Robert Langton, of Manchester, having faithfully reproduced the written characters referred to, we submit them to our readers as corroborations of our several averments that the street was originally named Lever-street ; that it derived its present mis-spelt name, between 1805 and 1816, from that local clerical celebrity, Parson Folds—not from any "fold" or close which thereabouts existed formerly—and that the posting of the name "Fold-street" on the opposite corner by the Bolton Corporation was another official error of judgment. Mr. "Thomas Smith, of Haulgh, farmer," had a representative present at the auction of the premises in Bradshawgate, who bid £350 for it, and he, being the highest bidder, was declared the purchaser at that sum, on Mr. Smith's behalf.

Accordingly by Indenture of Feoffment dated 1st May, 1806, Messrs. James Bayley and James Touchett, the surviving trustees and executors of the will of Dorning Rasbotham, deceased, in consideration of £350 paid to them, "bargained, sold, aliened, enfeoffed, and confirmed" unto the said Thomas Smith,* his heirs and assigns, "ALL THAT, the aforesaid Messuage, Burgage, or Dwelling-house, with the land, hereditaments, and appurtenances to the same belonging, and some time ago converted into two cottages or Dwelling-houses, situate and being on the west side of, and to the front of, a certain street within Bolton-le-Moors aforesaid, called and commonly known by the name of Bradshawgate, TOGETHER with the vacant land and appurtenances thereunto belonging, and then in the tenure, holding, or occupation of James Baron, as tenant thereof, or of his sub-tenants, and containing in the whole by admeasurement, including the scite of the buildings, 287 superficial square yards of land, or thereabouts, be the same more or less," &c. "To HOLD," &c., "for ever," &c. By a subsequent clause of the Deed Mr. Thomas Rushton, of Bolton-le-Moors, gentleman, was

---

* Thomas Smith, of the parish of Bolton, labourer and Mary Yates, of the parish of Middleton, spinster, were married in Bolton parish church by licence on the 29th of September, 1785, by Rev. E. Whitehead, vicar ; witnesses William Yates and John Bell. *Secondly*, Thomas Smith, of the parish of Bolton, widower, and Alice Smith, of the parish of Middleton, spinster, were married in Bolton parish church by licence on the 27th of January, 1791, by Rev. Jeremiah Gilpin, vicar ; witnesses William Smith and Peter Smith.

Mary, his first wife, was buried in Bolton parish churchyard 8th August, 1787.

appointed as attorney to deliver seizen of the premises to Thomas Smith, the purchaser. The signature of James Bayley, which betokens age, exceeding feebleness, or extreme nervousness, is witnessed by " Frances Bayley " and " William Eccles." The fluent signature of James Touchett is witnessed by the same William Eccles and " James Moorhouse." The receipt for the purchase money (£350) is signed and witnessed by the last two. A memorandum is endorsed signed by " Thomas Rushton," to the effect that " on the date of this deed peaceable possession of the hereditaments within mentioned was taken by Thomas Rushton, the attorney within named, who, after such possession taken, the like possession unto the within named Thomas Smith did give and deliver, To HOLD the same premises unto the said Thomas Smith, his heirs, and assigns, for ever, according to the true intent of the within written indenture, As WITNESS," &c.

Witnesses :—" JOHN SMITH,
SAMUEL VICKERS."

Soon after the date of the last mentioned deed of feoffment, a carrier's warehouse was erected, partly on the vacant land westwards of the present old building, and partly on the site of an outhouse belonging to the front messuage, by the feoffee Thomas Smith.

In 1816, Thomas Smith, the late purchaser, " being seized in his demesne as of fee " of the " messuage warehouse and hereditaments " in Bradshawgate, and having occasion for the sum of £600, agreed with John Heywood, of Little Bolton, cotton manufacturer, for the loan of that amount, upon the security of the whole of the premises. Accordingly by Indenture of Demise, by way of mortgage, dated 31st August, 1816, Thomas Smith, " of Haulgh, farmer," and Alice, his wife, in consideration of £600 paid to Thomas Smith by John Heywood, " granted, bargained, sold and demised " unto John Heywood, the premises comprised in the deed of 1806, words being added to the effect that same was then in the occupation of " Widow Pearson," her assigns or undertenants. " AND ALSO ALL THAT large carriers warehouse or building with the hereditaments and appurtenances thereunto belonging, now in the occupation of, and lately erected by, the said Thomas Smith, upon the said vacant land or some part thereof, and the scite, of one of the said two cottages or dwelling-houses, TOGETHER with the vacant land thereunto belonging, which said land and hereditaments hereby demised, including the scite of the said dwelling-house and warehouse, contain in the whole by a late admeasurement 287 superficial square yards of land or ground, or thereabouts, be the same more or less, AND ALL houses, outhouses, edifices, buildings, ways," &c. " To HOLD, &c., for 1000 years, YIELDING AND PAYING therefore yearly and every year during the said term, unto the said Thomas Smith, his heirs and assigns, the rent of one pepper corn on the 25th day of December in every year, if lawfully demanded," and subject to the proviso for redemption therein contained. The deed is signed by Thomas Smith and Alice* Smith, and witnessed by Robert Kay and James Bolling. A receipt for £600 is endorsed, signed by Thomas Smith, and attested by the same two witnesses. A bond for £1,200

* Second wife. See note on preceding page.

conditioned for payment of £600 and interest, collateral with that deed of mortgage, and of the same date, was executed by Thomas Smith, and attested by the same witnesses.

Thomas Smith, the mortgagor, died in May, 1817, aged 50, and was buried 25th of same month in Bolton parish churchyard. He left his son John Smith,* "of Haulgh, carrier," his heir-at-law, surviving him. Alice, his widow, died 4th February, 1825, aged 54.

The sum of £900 appears to have accumulated due to John Heywood, at the time of the death of Thomas, on foot of the mortgage security and Bond last described. John Smith, heir to the old premises and their incumbrances, being afterwards desirous of paying off that sum to John Heywood, contracted with Ellis Fletcher, of Clifton, a township adjoining Pendlebury, for a loan of £1,250, to enable him to do so, and "to answer his other occasions." Accordingly, by indenture dated 9th August, 1830, made between John Heywood of the first part, John Smith of the second part, and Ellis Fletcher of the third part, John Heywood, in consideration of £900, paid to him by Ellis Fletcher, by the direction of John Smith, and also in consideration of £350 paid by Ellis Fletcher to John Smith, "bargained, sold, and assigned," and the said John Smith also "granted, bargained, sold, assigned, ratified, and confirmed unto the said Ellis Fletcher, his executors, administrators and assigns," the premises comprised in the deed of 1806, words being added to show that they were then in the occupation of James Darbyshire. AND ALSO, &c. [the premises comprised in the mortgage of 1816.] "To HAVE AND TO HOLD, &c. unto the said Ellis Fletcher, his executors, administrators, and assigns, for all the rest residue, and remainder then to come and unexpired of the said term of 1,000 years, created by the said thereinbefore recited indenture of mortgage of the 31st day of August, 1816, without impeachment of waste, subject to the proviso or agreement thereinafter contained for redemption of the said premises," &c. The deed is signed by "John Heywood" and "John Smith," and witnessed by "R. A. Boardman." A receipt for £900 is signed by "John Heywood," and another for £350 is signed by "John Smith," both being witnessed by "R. A. Boardman."

Ellis Fletcher, by his will, dated 11th January, 1834, amongst other things, gave, devised, and bequeathed unto his brother, James Fletcher, Joseph Jones of Oldham, cotton spinner, Barton Fletcher Allen of Preston, gentleman, his (the testator's) son John Fletcher Ramsden, and his (testator's) wife, Mary Fletcher (whom he appointed his trustees), all the estates vested in him on any trust, or by way of mortgage, and which he had power to dispose of by that his will, with their appurtenances, unto the said trustees of that his will, their heirs, executors, administrators, and assigns, according to the nature and quality thereof respectively. UPON TRUST, &c. (as in such cases usual). Ellis Fletcher died on the 26th of April, 1834. His will was proved at Chester by

---

* John, son of Thomas Smith and Mary his (first) wife (daughter of John and Elizabeth Yates), born 18th July, 1786, baptized at the Unitarian Chapel, Bank-street, Bolton, on the 13th of August, 1786, by the Rev. John Holland, pastor.

Mary Fletcher and James Fletcher only, on the 11th December of that year. The same will was also proved at Canterbury on the 3rd February, 1835.

By a deed poll, dated 11th November, 1834, Joseph Jones, one of the trustees, renounced and declined the executorship and trusteeship. John Fletcher Ramsden (testator's son, who in his father's lifetime adopted the name of Ramsden in addition to his own), died 5th April, 1836. Mary Fletcher (testator's widow) died 13th April, 1836.

By indenture dated 27th April, 1836, James Fletcher, the acting surviving trustee, appointed John Moore of Bolton-le-Moors, surgeon, Jacob Fletcher Ramsden of Clifton, gentleman, Thomas Mulliner of Bolton-le-Moors, accountant, and Joseph Ramsden of Clifton, gentleman, to be new and co-trustees of the will of Ellis Fletcher.

By indenture of lease and release and assignment, dated 27th and 28th April, 1836, the release and assignment being made between James Fletcher of the first part, James Fletcher, John Moore, Jacob Fletcher Ramsden, Thomas Mulliner, and Joseph Ramsden of the second part, and Matthew Dawes of Bolton-le-Moors, gentleman [attorney], of the third part, James Fletcher "granted, bargained, sold, and released," &c., unto Matthew Dawes (in his actual possession then being, &c.), and to his heirs, "ALL the freehold manors, messuages, lands, tithes, rents, hereditaments and premises" mentioned in the said will, or purchased since the death of the said Ellis Fletcher in pursuance of the trusts of his will, and then vested in the said James Fletcher as trustee. AND all the estate, hereditaments, and premises, which were vested in the testator in trust or by way of mortgage, and all such as by virtue of his will, or by any subsequent conveyance, were then vested in James Fletcher by way of mortgage for securing any sum or sums of money belonging to the estate of the testator, and the reversion, &c. To HOLD the same unto Matthew Dawes and his heirs, To THE USE of the said James Fletcher, John Moore, Jacob Fletcher Ramsden, Thomas Mulliner, and Joseph Ramsden, their heirs and assigns, for ever, UPON the several trusts therein mentioned. And James Fletcher did thereby also bargain, sell, assign, transfer, and set over unto Matthew Dawes, his executors and administrators, ALL AND SINGULAR the manors, messuages, lands, tithes, rents, hereditaments, and premises, whatsoever and wheresoever, then vested in James Fletcher as trustee and executor of the said will, for any term or terms of years, chattel interest and interests, as well those which were vested in Ellis Fletcher as those which had since been assigned to or otherwise become vested in James Fletcher as such trustee and executor, including those whereof Ellis Fletcher was trustee or mortgagee, and those to which James Fletcher was as such trustee of the said will then mortgagee, &c. To HOLD, &c., unto M. Dawes, his executors, administrators and assigns, thenceforth for and during all the term and terms of years, interest or interests, for which the same were respectively held, then to come and unexpired thereof. UPON TRUST that Matthew Dawes should forthwith assign and make over all and singular the same premises, &c., unto James Fletcher, John Moore, Jacob Fletcher Ramsden, Thomas Mulliner, and Joseph Ramsden, their executors, administrators and assigns, UPON the several trusts therein mentioned.

D

By indenture, dated 28th April, 1836, endorsed upon the last mentioned indenture Matthew Dawes, " bargained, sold, assigned and set over," &c., unto James Fletcher, John Moore, Jacob Fletcher Ramsden, Thomas Mulliner, and Joseph Ramsden, their executors, administrators, and assigns, the premises assigned by " the within written indenture." To HOLD, &c. (usual words).

James Fletcher died 19th September, 1836. On the 23rd of September, 1837, letters of administration, with the will annexed, to the estate of Ellis Fletcher, unadministered by his widow and James Fletcher, were granted to Messrs. Moore, Mulliner, and Ramsden, the after appointed trustees.

John Smith, " common carrier," died intestate and unmarried on the 14th day of February, 1839, aged 52 years, and was buried on the 17th in Bolton parish churchyard. Being at the time of his death seized in fee of the premises in Bradshawgate, the same descended to and became vested in fee in William Smith,* his half-brother and heir at law, of Rumworth, yeoman. He also left another half-brother, Whittaker Smith,† of Haulgh Hall, common carrier, and two half-sisters, Jane Smith†† and Hannah Smith,‡ him surviving. William being desirous that the whole of the debts owing by John (except such part as the deceased's personal estate would enable his personal representatives to discharge) should be paid off out of the proceeds of the Bradshawgate premises, and being also desirous that his half-brother and half-sisters should each have an equal share along with himself therein, he agreed to convey and assure the same unto Whittaker Smith and Peter Smith ¶ (bookkeeper), their heirs and assigns, to such uses, upon such trusts, and for such ends, intents, and purposes as were declared by the next mentioned deed.

Accordingly by indentures of lease and release, dated 15th and 16th March, 1839, William Smith, for the nominal consideration of 10s., and also in consideration of the share thereinafter limited to him, and in further consideration of the natural love and affection which he had towards his brother and sisters, granted, &c., unto Whittaker and Peter Smith and their heirs, " FIRSTLY, ALL THAT Messuage or Dwelling-house, shop or shops, carrier's warehouse, and the land upon which the same were erected and built, situate in Bradshawgate and Folds'-street, within Bolton-le-Moors, in the said county, and also the vacant plot of land lying between the said messuage and dwelling-house, shop or shops, and the said carrier's warehouse," and all other the hereditaments and premises

* William Smith, son of Thomas and Alice Smith, born 28th February, and christened 27th March, 1792, by Rev. John Holland, minister of Bank-street Unitarian Chapel, Bolton.

† Whittaker Smith was born 27th March, christened 1st May, 1808, at Bank-street Unitarian Chapel, Bolton, by Rev. John Holland, pastor.

†† Jane Smith died 27th January, 1842, aged 48, and was buried in Bolton churchyard.

‡ In a declaration, dated 22nd February, 1850, Hannah Smith described herself as " Hannah Smith, of Haulgh Hall, in the township of Tonge-with-Haulgh, in the county of Lancaster, widow," and therein declares that " I am the daughter of Thomas Smith, late of Haulgh Hall aforesaid, common carrier, and Alice, his wife. My mother was the second wife of the said Thomas Smith."

¶ Born 1794.

conveyed and assured by the Deed of Feoffment of 1806, &c., and then in the several occupations of Whittaker Smith (as administrator of John Smith, deceased) and James Darbyshire and . . . . . (*sic*), as under tenants thereof. AND, SECONDLY, certain other property situate in Preston (not the subject of this documentary history), &c., TO HOLD, &c., for ever UPON TRUST as therein mentioned, to demise, sell, or mortgage the same, and out of the proceeds pay off such part of the debts of John Smith, deceased, as were due and owing, and which his personal estate was insufficient to discharge, and to divide the remainder equally between them. The deed is signed by William Smith, Whittaker Smith, and Peter Smith, and witnessed by " Richard Smith, farmer, Rumworth."

Whittaker Smith died 4th May, 1842, aged 34, and was buried on the 11th of the same month in Bolton parish church yard.

Peter Smith made a will dated 7th October, 1846, which contained the following devise :—" I devise all real estates (if any) vested in me as trustee or mortgagee to my said wife Hannah, my said cousin Peter Smith, and my said friend John Harwood, their heirs, executors, administrators and assigns for ever, subject to the equities affecting the same respectively." Testator appointed his wife, cousin, and friend so named, executrix and executors, and died on the 2nd December of the same year at Haulgh Hall, Tonge-with-Haulgh, aged 51¾. His will was proved on the 27th January of the following year at Chester, by his widow and the two executors.

It should be here stated, in view of the conveyance of the entire premises by the devisees of Peter Smith and others, that on the 20th of September, 1843, Her Majesty's Royal Licence and authority were granted to Jacob Fletcher Ramsden, one of the trust mortgagees, to drop the surname of Ramsden and to take and use the surname and arms of Fletcher only, whereby his name became Jacob Fletcher Fletcher.

Joseph Ramsden died 25th July, 1848, leaving John Moore, Jacob Fletcher Fletcher, and Thomas Mulliner his co-trustees and co-mortgagees surviving him.

By Indenture dated 12th November, 1849, made between John Moore of Bolton, Esq., Jacob Fletcher Fletcher of Peel Hall, Esq., and Thomas Mulliner of Bolton, accountant, of the first part, Hannah Smith of Haulgh, widow, Peter Smith of Manchester, agent, and John Harwood of Bolton, corn dealer, of the second part, and Thomas Walmsley, of Bolton, ironmonger, of the other part, IT WAS WITNESSED that in consideration of £1,000 to Messrs. Moore, Fletcher, and Mulliner, at the request and by the direction of Hannah Smith, Peter Smith, and John Harwood, in full satisfaction of all money owing on the Indenture of Mortgage of 9th August, 1830, and also in consideration of £200 to Hannah Smith, Peter Smith, and John Harwood, making together the agreed purchase money of the premises paid by Thomas Walmsley, they, the said Messrs. Moore, Fletcher, and Mulliner thereby assigned, surrendered, and yielded up, and Hannah Smith, Peter Smith, and John Harwood granted, bargained, sold, aliened, and conveyed unto Thomas Walmsley " ALL THAT messuage or dwelling-house, shop, and carrier's warehouse, situate in Bradshawgate and Folds'-street, within Bolton-le-Moores aforesaid, AND ALSO the vacant plot of land lying between the said messuage or dwelling-house and the said carrier's warehouse, the site of all which premises contains in the whole 287 superficial square yards of land, or thereabouts, be the same more or less, as the same premises were formerly in the possession of the said John Smith and of James Darbyshire, and are now in the occupation of . . . . . . [blank in original deed as tenant thereof. And all outhouses, dwellings, &c., &c., To HAVE AND TO HOLD, &c., for ever." The deed is signed by "John Moore," "J. Fletcher Fletcher," "Thomas Mulliner," "Hannah Smith," "Peter Smith," and "John Harwood," and attested as to the signatures of Hannah Smith and John Harwood, by "Christopher Briggs, solicitor, Bolton;" as to that of Peter Smith, by "W. R. Jackson, solicitor, Bolton;" as to the signatures of John Moore and Thomas Mulliner, by "John Sudren, clerk to Messrs. Briggs & Jackson, solicitors, Bolton;" and as to the signature of Jacob Fletcher Fletcher, by "Joseph Gerrard, clerk with Mr. Dawes, solicitor, Bolton." A receipt for £200, the portion of the purchase money payable to Hannah Smith, Peter Smith, and John Harwood, is duly signed by them.

The course of leasing, re-leasing, inheriting, selling, mortgaging, and again selling, having gone on somewhat tamely through the hands of successive conveyancing lawyers, during the 170 years embraced by the foregoing portion of the title deeds, it could scarcely be expected that the venerable old wood and plaster building could much longer escape the attention of the chancery practitioners. Eventually the opportunity offered, and the little suit of "Alice Fletcher, an infant, and Ann Fletcher, an infant, by Peter Higson, their next friend, PLAINTIFFS; John Moore, Thomas Mulliner, and Jacob Fletcher Fletcher, and Ellis Fletcher, DEFENDANTS," was commenced by petition on the 13th of December, 1849. So far as the venerable premises and Mr. Thomas Walmsley, the purchaser, were thereby affected, the suit was a mere brush, inasmuch as, in simple obedience to an order of the vice-chancellor, he paid the involved portion of his purchase money—£1,000 and interest—to, and obtained a receipt from, the Governor and Company of the Bank of England, and left the litigious infants to attain their majority and the lodgment as best they might, and at same time relieved Madame Wood and Plaster and the adjoining premises of the incubus of a very sticky mortgage.

During the succeeding quarter of a century the property remained solely in the hands of Mr. Walmsley, the purchaser, who, meanwhile, built a large warehouse, over the site of the partly demolished carriers' warehouse, and partly on a portion of the vacant ground westwards of the rear of the old relic. Tho latter continued as before to be tenanted, sometimes as one shop, and at other times as two, according to the commercial calibres of those who ventured upon its tenancy during that period.

On the 5th April, 1873, Mr. Walmsley granted a lease of the old messuage and premises to Mr. Johnson Mills, of Bolton, auctioneer, for 999 years, from 12th May, 1873, at the annual rent of £45. 10s. The description of the premises in that document are;—"ALL THAT plot of land situate within the

Borough of Bolton aforesaid, as the same is delineated and described with respect to the boundaries and admeasurement thereof, in the plan drawn in the margin of these presents and comprised within the space edged with pink in the same plan, and containing in area 124] superficial square yards or thereabouts, be the same more or less; and bounded on the north side thereof by Folds-street, and containing on that side 43 feet 3 inches; on the east side thereof by Bradshawgate, and containing on that side 25 feet 11 inches; on part of the south side thereof by premises belonging to the trustees and executors of Thomas Chantler, deceased; and on the remaining part by the wall hereinafter mentioned (the same wall being coloured blue on the said plan), and containing on the part of that side adjoining the said premises of the said trustees and executors 33 feet 9 inches, and on the remaining part thereof 6 feet 10 inches; and on the west side thereof by other premises of the said Thomas Walmsley, and containing on part cf that side 12 feet 5 inches, and then (after running 10 inches in a westerly direction) on the remaining part of that side 14 feet 4 inches, be the said several dimensions more or less. AND ALSO ALL THAT messuage or dwelling-house, and the shops now in the respective occupation of Moses Barron, as tenant thereof; AND all other the erections and buildings erected and now standing thereon. AND ALSO all the estate and interest, if any, of the said Thomas Walmsley (but according to such estate, and not by way of warranty), of and in all that the said wall delineated and described on the aforesaid plan, and thereon coloured blue, the site whereof contains in area one-half of a square yard or thereabouts, together with the appurtenances thereunto belonging."

By Indenture of Assignment, dated 23rd July, 1879, Mr. Johnson Mills assigned to councillor Thomas Bromley, of Folds'-street, Bolton, the premises so derived by him under the Indenture of 5th April, 1873, for the remainder of the said term of 999 years. In this deed the tenants of the old building are described as " Mr. Duckworth and another." The premises have been for some time vacant, preparatory to demolition. The businesses carried on by the last two occupiers were those of a tobacconist on a small scale, and a tripe dealer. *Sic transit gloria mundi!* On the site, when cleared, Mr. Bromley will, early in the next spring, erect a magnificent Fine Art Gallery and Artists' Repository, to which he means to remove the business presently carried on by him at the opposite corner of Folds-street and Bradshawgate.

Unwilling that this vestige of old Bolton should be quite lost to his townsmen by its complete demolition, Mr. Bromley, in August last, resolved to make a presentation of the materials to the town, provided some local gentlemen would come forward and make arrangements for the removal and reconstruction of the fabric in some convenient position in the borough park, or other suitable place in or in the neighbourhood of Bolton, as a memento of bygone street architecture. A direct offer having been made to the Bolton Corporation by Mr. Bromley to place the materials at their disposal, the Park and Burial Board Committee, at their meeting on Thursday, 4th September last, duly considered the matter, but declined to accept the " white elephant." The resolution arrived at was, " That the thanks of the Committee be tendered to

Mr. Councillor Bromley for the offer made by him of the building at the corner of Folds-street and Bradshawgate, and they regret that they are unable to accept such offer." Early in the spring its demolition will be proceeded with. Through the courtesy of Mr. Bromley, we shall be permitted to arrange for a close antiquarian vigil over the site during the progress of the work, and should any " finds " reward us for our pains, they will be duly chronicled and illustrated in a future number of this magazine. At all events, we shall have something more to say concerning the " fossils " to be turned over. Some rare relic of the siege of Bolton may perchance be unearthed!

(Short architectural description, and brief chronological review of successive tenants, in our next issue.)

COLLECTANEA; OR, WHAT THE RECORDS SAY.

UNDER this head we mean to reproduce, *verbatim* and *in extenso*, the text of selected Records and ancient Documents illustrative of local history, and especially of those which most concern the territory embraced by the title of our new magazine. It is known that many such documents and manuscripts exist in various repositories, public and private, but they remain as sealed books to nearly all, save their custodians. Favoured chroniclers have ever drawn historical materials from these sources of information, but the privileged writers seem to have been more anxious to amalgamate selections from such gleanings with others collected elsewhere, than to disclose details which the general writer wisely enough imagined could only interest local readers. Our desire to disseminate the entire contents of such records or documents through the medium of this magazine will, we trust, be duly appreciated by our readers, We do not by any means aim at a cheap method of filling its pages, as we shall, on the contrary, be obliged to circumscribe the space to be occupied monthly with such matter, and besides, in nine cases out of ten, as is known by the initiated, the expense attendant upon transcripts of such documents is, as a rule, excessive. We are, however, happy to say that our negotiations, with a view to gaining access to, or obtaining copies of miscellaneous historical manuscripts deposited in the various public offices, to be reproduced in these columns have been met in a fair spirit by a high official; and on going to press we are happy to announce the conclusion of most satisfactory arrangements for accomplishing that end. The suggestions of subscribers and contributors with reference to the selection of future transcripts, will at all times meet with our best attention.

BOUNDARIES.

U NDER this head we shall reproduce the text of ancient descriptions of the "meres and bounds" of parishes and townships. In each succeeding issue we shall describe the boundaries of one or other of the parishes or townships which come within the range of the title of our magazine. By way of identification of the local topography of the period to which each such ancient description is assigned, and as a fitting contrast thereto, each reproduction will be followed, where practicable, by authentic details of the boundaries at the present time.

PARISH OF ASHTON-UNDER-LYNE.[*] —Description of the boundaries of the parish in 1643, noted after a perambulation had taken place :—

" Whereas the boundary of the sayde parish of Ashton-under-Lyne begins at the boundary mark at Cross Bank, above Hey, near Austerlands, at the north extremity of the said parish ; and so descending to the west by Mylne Bottom, where it meets the little Medlock, and so following that little water down to Leese, dividing it from Ouldham, and turning south-westerly to Holt's, where it leaves the brook, goes west by Turfpits down another rill to Cherry Valley, where it ascends north-west to near a place called Glodwick Clough, where it turns west by Fitton Hill to Copster Hill, by Oak, Lyme, and down by another rill called Medlock, to a place by Cutler Hill, called Cat Alley, where it meets the main Medlock, and so ascending the main brook Medlock in the hamlet of Woodhouses, it goes south by Buckley Hill, to the edge of the Moss, and so on by or betwixt Ashton Moss and Droylsden Moss side, to below Audenshaw, near Corn Hill, abutting on Openshagh, Goreton, Denton, and Haughton, and so on below Hooley Hill, to the river of Tame, and so ascending the river of Tame, by Shepley Demesne, to Willows, Knotts at Brook, and so betweene Ashton Town to Dukinfield, all the way to Mab Holes, and following the divers windings of the said Tame, to the bridge of Staley dividing Lancashire and Cheshire, and ascending from the sayde bridge of Stayley by Stayley in Cheshire on the one hand, and Gleut, Herrod, Sour Acre, Scout Mill, and to Bottoms on the Ashton hand, where the devycons of Lancashire, Yorkshire, and Cheshire meete, in Mossley Hamlett, in Ashton, in Mickelhurst-under-Tyntwisel, in Cheshire, and in Quick Mere, in the lordship of Saddelword ; and so ascending a brook of the said Tame to the north-west, betweene Mossley and Quick Hamletts, below Lyght Birches, and so on to Thornleigh and to Highe Knowls, where it meetes again with the little Medlock, and crossing it by Ashes, by Lees, to the abutment on Hey Chapel, and so ascending the hill to the boundary stone of Cross Bank, the first boundary or meare."

---

[*] Until the year 1291 the territory which is now the extensive parish of Ashton-under-Lyne, was part of the ancient parish of Manchester. The latter was constituted soon after the founding of York Cathedral by Oswald, King of Northumbria.

OUR MONTHLY CONVERSAZIONE.

UNDER this heading we shall register such items of archæological, historical, and genealogical "intelligence," as may come within the lines or scope of our project. The matter will be divided into two sections—" LOCAL," as applied to places within the territory embraced by our title, and " GENERAL," as referable to places beyond those limits, or to the country at large.

LOCAL.

MANCHESTER.—Mr. F. Madox Brown lately finished the second cartoon of the series of illustrations of the history of Manchester, which he has been commissioned to execute in the Town Hall of that city. The work is named, " The Romans at Mancenion," and depicts the building of a fort or castrum near the present site of Manchester. In the centre of the design stands a Roman military engineer, displaying to the commander of the legion a plan of the fort which is being built. The large scroll is open in the hands of its designer. The officer, wearing a dragon-crested helmet and scarlet mantle, turns a little sideways to the front, thus shewing his face, while he studies the fortifications with the aid of the plan. The robe of the engineer is blown out behind his figure by the breeze which rushes past the heights, the bleakness of which is suggested by the thick clothing of the wife of the commander, who attends him, and wears thick furs and woollens. She holds by the hand her sturdy boy of eight years old, who, with a toy clarion in his hand, and with sportive energy of the Roman sort, kicks out behind at the face of a burly negro, a legionary, who, standing on a lower platform than that occupied by the principal figures, barely escapes a blow, and turns to the brutal boy with a diffident grin. British labourers are occupied on the walls, bringing materials, hewn stones, and mortar, which Roman soldiers, clad in armour because of the cold, are arranging on the rising walls. From this high point we survey the winding course of the river which is now called the Medlock, and to its banks beyond over the fosse of the camp.

MANCHESTER. — Several schemes were lately under consideration with respect to the future of the Oldham-street Wesleyan Chapel site and premises in this city. One was that the present chapel, which is far larger than existing needs require, should be taken down, a smaller one built, and suitable connexional premises erected at the rear. Another was that one-half the site which fronts Oldham-street should be sold, and the money thus raised employed in erecting chapel, conference hall, and offices on the other half of the site which faces Spear-street. A third scheme was that which proposes to sell the whole site at Oldham-street, on which chapel, vestries, chapel committee-rooms, &c., now stand, and to purchase a site elsewhere, on which a smaller and more suitable chapel should be erected, and also to find convenient premises for the officers of the chapel committee. It was finally resolved by the committee appointed for the purpose by the late Wesleyan Conference that Conference be recommended to sell the whole of the site on which the Oldham-street Chapel and premises now stand, and to build a chapel for the Oldham-street circuit at a convenient place. If this resolution be accepted by the Conference, the best known Methodist centre in Manchester, and indeed in the north of England, will be known only to history.

MANCHESTER.—At a meeting of the Council of Owens College, held in the afternoon of Friday, 17th October last, an interesting present was received from the executors of the late Mr. Samuel Faulkner (a former partner of Mr. John Owens) in the shape of a characteristic kit-kat portrait of the founder's father, Mr. Owen Owens. The portrait, without any pretensions to high excellency, is soundly painted, and evidently faithfully presents the ruddy and cheerful features of a small-statured, stout old gentleman of Welsh origin. There is no date to the picture, but as we find that the artist, William Lovatt, flourished in Manchester as a "portrait and miniature painter," first at 5, Faulkner-street, afterwards at 7, Coupland-street, Greenheys, between the years 1832-8, it is natural to assume that the portrait was painted about that period, especially as Mr. Owen Owens resided in Nelson-street, Oxford Road, in close proximity to the artist's abode in Coupland-street. Mr. Owen Owens was 80 years old when he died, on the 16th January, 1844, so that he would be about 70 years of age when the portrait was taken, which will now adorn the Senate-room of his son's famous college. Touching the painter, there is a smack of romance hitherto unchronicled in the history of Manchester artists. He came here from Ashover, in Derbyshire. His brother Charles was at that time a well-known tobacconist in Market-street. About 1838-9 the artist suddenly disappeared, and his whereabouts was a perfect mystery, even to his brother, who, however, upon his death, in 1850, left him a legacy, to be paid by his successor and executor, Mr. Bevins. But from the day he left Manchester until the present no tidings of him have been received. In connection with the father's portrait, it may be mentioned in passing that there is no portrait in existence of the founder of the College, except a very beautifully executed medallion by Woolner, from a silhouette presented some time ago by Mrs. Faulkner, which has not been hitherto publicly noticed. It hangs in a conspicuous place over the fireplace of the Senate-house.

MANCHESTER.—The *Manchester City News* continues to maintain its *prestige* as chief amongst those Lancashire journals whose editors wisely reserve portions of their space weekly for contributed Notes, Answers, Comments, and Queries in the departments of local history, tradition, philology, and antiquity. Nearly a whole page of the paper is now occupied weekly by interesting matter of this class. The quarterly reprints of such contributions in book form, at a mere nominal price, are valuable additions to our county literature. The eighth part of these reprints will be due shortly.

BOLTON.—At the inaugural dinner given on Saturday, 27th September last, in the new warehouse of Messrs. Lever & Co. (erected on the south-west side of the Town Hall Square, Bolton, on a site formerly known as Howell Croft), Mr. Lever, referring to the history of the Manor-street (formerly called Bank-street) establishment, described the latter as "the *oldest* wholesale grocery house in the town." What says "the oldest inhabitant" to this?

Bolton.—The "Green" memorial window in St. Matthew's Church, Bolton, was completed early in November last, and inaugurated on the 9th of that month, when the Bishop of the diocese preached in the morning. It is a modest though rich window, exquisitely sweet in harmony, delicate and almost ethereal in colouring, whilst the drapery of the various figures is graceful in the highest degree. The tracery is warm in its tone, various rich tints being beautifully blended. There is a circle imitative of the rose in the upper part, whose centre is filled with the dove as the emblem of the Holy Spirit. Around are the emblems of the four Evangelists. In the *feuilles* against the grand rose are placed the "Alpha" and "Omega," the beginning and the end of all things, and below four angels in a position of adoration. The five large lights of the window are devoted to a representation of the Ascension of our Lord to heaven. This is arranged in two tableaux, the lower one representing the Apostles stead-fastly gazing up into heaven, rapt and wondering, as if they would penetrate the clouds which hide their Master from their sight; the upper one pictorially describes the reception of Christ beyond the skies by the heavenly host. The figure of the Saviour is exceptionally noble, and the attendant angels are grouped around Him, manifestly receiving Him with every mark of honour, their tongues uttering joyful alleluias. Altogether the window is a splendid specimen of artistic work in stained glass, and reflects the greatest credit upon the artist, Monsieur Jean Baptiste Capronnier, of the Rue Rogier, Brussels. On a plate band at the base of the window are inscribed the suggestive words, "To the glory of God and the cherished memory of John Green, a great benefactor to this church and parish, who died March 4th, 1879." The cost was £240.

Bolton.—During the past forty-six weeks each successive issue of the *Bolton Weekly Journal* contained a serial instalment of "Half-hours among the Tombs, or Bolton Records of the Past," by an anonymous author, being a reproduction of the tombstone literature of Bolton old parish church and churchyard. Judi-ciously interspersed among these are highly interesting and carefully written comments upon the positions of the tombstones, and the peculiarities of their inscriptions, with occasional biographical notices of the deceased. Genealogically viewed the work is replete with materials for future biographers of Bolton worthies. Moreover, in this case, the importance of the author's labours becomes enhanced tenfold when it is understood that not a single inscription among the 333 which have been reproduced verbatim in the *Journal* is now to be seen by visitors to the church or churchyard. At the time of the demoli-tion of Bolton old church, after the pews had been removed, about 133 tomb-stones were found overlying the vaults below, and overspreading the floors of the chancel, nave, and aisles. These were removed temporarily, and subse-quently relaid on the eve of the completion of the new church, in or near their old sites. Other tombstones, numbering about two hundred, which formerly bordered the south, east, and west walls of the old church, were embraced within the extended area of the new church, and became also lost to view. That section of the series which embraces these buried tombstones is also valuable from an antiquarian point of view, as until the present new parish church become a ruin they are hermetically sealed against inspection, under the floor of the new church. Allusions having occasionally been made by the author, in the section published, to future portions of his work to be headed " Displaced Tombstones," " Monuments," " Tablets," " Brasses," " Memorial Windows," &c., we may expect further interesting instalments of the series. The whole of the thousands of tombstones which cover the immense area of the parish churchyard will, it appears, be treated by the author, but probably his labours in this section will be confined to the more ancient among the number, and such of the modern inscriptions as may be accounted important. We understand that the publication of the remainder of the manuscript in the columns of the *Journal* will extend over the greater part of the year 1880. We refer with the greatest satisfaction and pleasure to these combined efforts of a spirited publisher and his unwearying contributor to rescue the buried, or, as the author puts it, " interned " tombstones from the artificial oblivion which befell them on the occasion of the destruction of the old church. The entire series will prove an invaluable fund of information, placed cut-and-dry at the finger ends of those who may require local materials for biographical or historical purposes. The surprising intimacy with which the author alludes to and deals with all matters and things connected with the old and new churches and churchyard, and the technical skill displayed in the descriptive matter, must convince readers of his preparedness to bring his prodigious task to a successful termination.

BARTON-UPON-IRWELL.—Mr. Robert Langton, the eminent Manchester engraver, informs us that a discovery of some interest has just been made by a working man while pulling down the old hall at Barton-upon-Irwell. " I can," he says, " get no definite information as to the extent of the ' find,' but an earthen vessel was found containing silver coins, and having seen some twenty of these coins I can describe them. They consist of shillings, sixpences, and groats of Elizabeth, James the First, and Charles the First. The mint marks are a rose, an anchor, and the ' tun ' of Throckmorton, master of the mint. From the latest coins being of the reign of Charles the First, the vessel was probably deposited where found about the middle of the seventeenth century, during the Civil Wars. The coins are much worn, and several of the sixpences ' crooked,' or purposely bent, telling plainly of some old love-making."

LEIGH.—About two columns weekly of *The Leigh Chronicle* are set apart for Antiquarian and Genealogical Notes, under the title of " The Chronicle Scrap Book."

BURY.—Under the head of " Notes and Queries," interesting communications from contributors appear weekly in the *Bury Times*, chiefly on subjects connected with local tradition, history, and folk-lore.

TURTON TOWER.—We understand that some carefully-culled notes on this ancient mansion and its successive owners, commencing from the earliest period and brought down to the present time, are on the eve of publication in book form, and may be expected to appear early in the new year. We have been favoured with a perusal of some of the proof sheets, and we are therefore in a position to state that it relates facts, the collection of which are the result of diligent search and study, and eminently calculated to render the work a desirable addition to works on local Lancashire history. The matter abounds with dates, names, and important *data*. On the more obscure points several authorities are quoted, whilst certain contradictory assertions made by well-known historians are cleverly discussed, with the view of clearing away doubts. The ancient objects found in the interior of the tower being described in a matter-of-fact, yet none the less interesting, way, this portion will prove a great treat for those who may never have been fortunate enough to obtain a personal inspection of the objects on the spot. The last chapter is devoted to the relation of several "ghost stories" associated with the tower and neighbourhood, which will, in the estimation of many, agreeably diversify the contents. An important feature is an accompanying original illustration of the tower, in the four corners of which the "arms," &c., of the principal owners of the old edifice are represented. A sketch is also given of the memorable iron-bound "coffer," the dumb witness of an extraordinary disturbance between a lady of the Orrell family and her eldest son in the latter part of the sixteenth century. The publication, which will well merit the support of all who interest themselves in local antiquity, is entitled "Notes on Turton Tower and its Successive Owners," and will, we have no doubt, reflect credit upon its author and compiler—Mr. James C. Scholes, of Bolton.

GENERAL.

LIVERPOOL.—The Historic Society of Lancashire and Cheshire, which was established in 1848, and holds its meetings in Liverpool, has not for the last few years been in the flourishing condition that could be desired for the only learned society in the county devoting itself exclusively to archæological investigations. Indeed it was recently proposed to wind it up altogether. An effort is being made to reconstruct it, and there is every probability of success. The Society has published thirty-one volumes, and these contain many contributions of importance from Messrs. R. G. Latham, A. Hume, C. Hardwick, J. Harland, H. A. Bright, A. Craig Gibson, J. Mayer, T. T. Wilkinson, and other well-known antiquaries. A considerable portion of the papers, however, are not of the character that might be expected in the transactions of a purely historic society, but include disquisitions on political economy and natural science. In future it is proposed to concentrate the efforts of the Association upon strictly archæological and historical lines, devoting especial attention to the memorials of the past history of the two counties. The impetus that has been given to historical study within the last few years warrants the hope that the society will be abundantly successful in following up this new department. For the present session papers have been promised by Mr. T. G. Rylands, F.S.A. (the president), Father Gibson, Mr. J. P. Earwaker (editor of *Local Gleanings*), Mr. J. O. Rylands, and other local antiquaries. A certain melancholy interest attached to the paper announced for a late meeting, as it was a contribution by the late Rev. Daniel H. Haigh, whose death has been a notable loss to Anglo-Saxon scholarship.

DUBLIN.—*Saunders' Daily News-Letter*, the oldest newspaper in Ireland, expired on Monday, 24th November last.

LEYLAND.— Her Majesty's royal licence and authority were given in September last to "Thomas Townley Parker, of Cuerden Hall, in the parish of Leyland, of Astley, in the parish of Chorley, of Royle and of Entwistle, both in the parish of Whalley, all in the county palatine of Lancaster," to use henceforth "the surname of Townley in addition to and before that of Parker, and to bear the arms of Townley quartered with those of Parker."

LATELY a series of attractive articles, entitled "Strange Stories, Scenes, Mysteries, and Characters in our National and Local History," was commenced in the columns of the *Hull Miscellany*, a very entertaining and well-arranged little work, exceedingly popular in the chief towns on the Humber, of which William Andrews, Esq., F.R.H.S., is the editor. Each paper contains much curious, valuable, and out-of-the-way information—the result of laborious research and keen discrimination. The fidelity with which the writer clings to fact tends to heighten the interest so conspicuously manifested by readers, who eagerly await each instalment of his historic romance, and who ever increase in numbers. In other walks and works Mr. Andrews displays unalloyed antiquarian tastes of the highest order, and in the most ubiquitous manner. The works to which his prolific pen has contributed are legion. We are happy to announce that he has kindly promised to place *Old South-East Lancashire* on the list of recipients of his archæological and historical favours. Respecting maces, Mr. Andrews says :—We have gleaned some curious notes. Dr. Clarke considers the use of the mace by corporations to be derived from the ceremonies attendant on the preservation of Agamemnon's sceptre by the Chæroneans, B.C. 1201. Our readers will remember that when Cromwell was forcibly dissolving the Long Parliament, April 20, 1653, he said, pointing to the symbol of the Speaker's authority, "Remove that fool's bauble !" The mace was melted down and sold by order of the House of Commons. We find in the *History of Leicester*, by the late James Thompson, F.S.A., particulars of a singular Leicester custom. In 1766 we are told that a Mr. Fisher was elected mayor. According to Mr. Thompson's able work, "Mr. Fisher was one of the few remaining Jacobites who were always ready to manifest their aversion to the reigning dynasty when occasion offered. It was the invariable custom of the newly-elected Mayor, previous to his election, to proceed (in accordance with the requirements of the charter of James the First) to the Castle, on the Monday after Martinmas Day, there to take an oath, before the Steward of the Duchy of Lancaster, to perform well and faithfully all and every ancient custom, and so forth, according to the best of his knowledge. When Mr. Mayor and his attendants arrived at a certain place within the precincts of the Castle, the bearer of the great mace lowered it from its upright position, in token of acknowledgment to the superior authority of the ancient feudal earls within their own stronghold. This ceremony was purposely omitted when Mayor Fisher attended at the Castle gateway, the town servant refusing to 'slope the mace,' as it was designated. The Constable of the Castle, or his deputy, therefore refused admission to the civic functionary. After that date the Mayor went in private to the Castle to comply with the terms of the ancient charter."

THE last survivor of the eight who signed that notable document "THE PEOPLE'S CHARTER" was John Arthur Roebuck, M.P. for Sheffield, who died at his London residence early on the morning of Sunday, 30th November last. He was born at Madras in 1802; was grandson of Dr. John Roebuck, of Sheffield; and was maternally descended from the poet Tickell.

ON the morning of Sunday, 7th inst. (December, 1879), John Wesley's celebrated chapel in the City Road, London, historically known throughout the world as the Cathedral of Methodism, was almost entirely destroyed by fire, originating in the overheating of the warming apparatus. The historic building "Wesley's Morning Chapel" was gutted, and the main chapel, holding 2,000 persons, was greatly injured. The elaborate monuments—one to Dr. Waddy, father of the late M.P. for Barnstaple, and valued at £1,000— were also damaged, and the beautiful frescoed ceiling was irreparably injured, but Wesley's pulpit was saved.

₊ We beg to acknowledge our indebtedness to the Editors of the *Manchester Guardian, Manchester City News, Buxton Advertiser, High Peak News,* and some other provincial papers which we have not seen, for their kindly references to the preliminary announcement of our intention to start this magazine.

OBITUARY.

RAWSON.—Mr. Henry Rawson, J.P., Prestwich Lodge, died 26th November last. He was one of the original proprietors of the *Manchester Examiner and Times*, as he was also of the defunct *London Morning Star*, with which newspaper Mr. John Bright was associated. He was born at Nottingham, and was in his sixty-first year.

ORMEROD.—Mr. Oliver Ormerod died at his residence in Roach Place, Rochdale, on 1st November last. He was amongst the first of those whose goods were seized and sold for refusing to pay the church-rate, when the Rev. W. R. Hay, of Peterborough notoriety, was vicar of the Rochdale Parish Church. He was one of the contributors to a magazine which was entitled the *Vicar's Lantern*, and in 1844 edited the *Spectator*, a local periodical, in which he wrote a series of humorous articles, entitled "Yeomanry Papers." In 1851 he published another amusing production, written in the Lancashire dialect, entitled "Th' Felley fro Rachda's Visit too the Greyte Egg-shibishun."

BOWES.—The death of Mr. Robert Aitken Bowes, editor of the *Bolton Guardian*, took place on 7th November last, at his residence, 21, Halliwell New Road, Bolton, in the 43rd year of his age. He was a son of the late Mr. John Bowes, an eminent religious controversialist, and evangelist of the society known as the Christian Brethren, who also occupied the position of editor of the *Truth Promoter*, a publication issued in the interests of the sect with which he was connected. The subject of our notice was born at Dundee, but passed his early days at Manchester, working as a printer. He afterwards proceeded to Dundee, where, along with his brother, he printed and published the *Truth Promoter*, edited by his father. In 1863 Mr. Bowes came to Bolton and filled the position of reporter at the *Guardian* office. About ten years ago, he undertook the editorial management of the paper. As a journalist he was painstaking and energetic.

TO CORRESPONDENTS AND CONTRIBUTORS.

R. R. (Rochdale) and other Inquirers.—You may save yourselves the unnecessary trouble of recopying your sketches if of a size too large for our pages. Our engraver is in a position to photograph any size of sketch or object upon the wood, and by means of the lens effect any needful reduction of scale.

The "STANDLEY BARN CHARITY" and the "SALFORD CHAPEL CHARITY," commonly called "THE BOOTH CHARITIES."—This article is unavoidably held over until our next issue.

PARISH CLERK.—Yes. You, and all other parish clerks within the Hundred of Salford, will benefit yourselves and us by putting yourselves upon corresponding terms with the editor.

YOUNG OLDHAM.—The following old obituary notice gives the information you require:—"Lately, at Loeside, near Oldham, James Ogden, aged 81. It is worthy of remark that he was born, lived, and died at the same place; and was uncle, great uncle, and great-great uncle to 147 persons."—*Manchester Mercury and Harrop's General Advertiser, Tuesday, 22nd January,* 1805.

departure from the main track, in which the general writer ever was and is compelled to move, we hope to localise our publication, while by entering into those details which past and contemporaneous writers of the general class were and are obliged to reject, we hope to arrive at a clearer comprehension of the myriads' of local facts, circumstances, and traditions, the general tenour of which is seldom more than superficially, or it may be imperfectly, understood by those beyond their immediate *locale*. To enable us to investigate local subjects successfully, we desire the co-operation of at least one zealous correspondent in each township within our titular district. The names of such townships appear upon the border of the front page of our wrapper. Through the instrumentality of an organisation of this sympathetic character, hidden materials may be brought to light, scanty facts augmented, discoveries investigated, inquiries prosecuted, documents inspected, and veracities tested : while the weaving together of facts thus elicited may be performed broadly, under the full assurance that the value and utility of the web were mainly regulated by the proportion of truth used in the texture of its warp, and the discrimination exercised in the manipulation of its weft. The first step of the ablest historians—general or local—is one of investigation. Humbly following this standard example, we announce publicly that equitable acknowledgments will be given for approved literary contributions. Original pencil or ink sketches or photographs illustrative of accompanying manuscripts will be similarly recognised; if rejected they will be returned. Those of the "Notes and Queries" class, readers' "Suggestions," "Answers," and "Gleanings," if of local character, will be specially welcomed. Information as to "finds" or discoveries should be communicated to the editor, in order that prompt examination and investigation may follow. We have made arrangements for the occasional reproduction of pedigrees of noted Lancashire families, brought down to the present time. It will, however, be observed that the genealogical department of the magazine will not be confined to special articles or detailed pedigrees. Every opportunity afforded by the mere mention in any article of the name of any local worthy or family will, as a rule, be embraced for the purpose of adding a brief genealogical comment or footnote with respect to such individual or family.

An attempt having been made to render the permanent illustrations on the wrapper and title-page self-explanatory of the present and future contents of the magazine, and of the general aim of the promoter, we cannot do better than permit them to fulfil their purpose, without further comment. No wish to make capital out of the magazine has yet entered our minds. On the contrary, we shall be highly pleased indeed should it become self-supporting, and instrumental in reducing our largely accumulated store of historical materials and gleanings, and increasing—in a corresponding degree—the historical knowledge of the readers of South-East Lancashire. Any profit derived from the publication of the magazine will be devoted to the increase in number of its pages and illustrations, and improvement of the general contents.

We are indebted to Mr. Robert Langton, of No. 1, Fennel-street, Manchester, our engraver, for the gifted readiness with which he caught and carried out our ideas with respect to our permanent illustrations, and the fidelity and expedition with which he executed the two engravings illustrative of an accompanying article; to Mr. W. F. Tillotson, proprietor of the *Bolton Evening News*, for the preparation of the intricate typographical stereotype which borders the front page of our wrapper; and to the proprietors of the *Manchester Guardian*, for the promptness and efficiency with which their large share in the work of production of our first number was performed.

To Subscribers.

Annual Subscribers, who pay 12s. in advance, will be entitled to have early copies of the magazine forwarded monthly to any address within the United Kingdom, *post free*. Post-office orders (or value in postage stamps) to be made payable to Mr. J. F. Matthews, Swinton, near Manchester. Early orders for single copies of future numbers are requested, as a limited number only will be printed monthly.

All communications to be addressed to Mr. J. F. Matthews, 106, Manchester Road (near the Market Place), Swinton.

Swinton, 19th December, 1879.

www.ingramcontent.com/pod-product-compliance
Lightning Source LLC
Chambersburg PA
CBHW032138080426
42733CB00008B/1122